Still

Mila Cuda

Still

Cover design and layout by Tiffany Chu

Edited by Ally Ang and Josh Savory

Formatted by Josh Savory

www.gameoverbooks.com

Key

In 2017, my New Year's resolution was to write a poem each day. This is the only resolution I've ever kept; I now regard it as a grave yet fascinating mistake. Overwhelmed by the quantity, these poems exist as unedited fragments of my daily life on the brink of 18-year-old adulthood. The poems entitled Resolution X come directly from that experiment, as do many of the floating excerpts throughout the collection.

◇✦◇

For the past few years, I have been working on a series of digital collage poems made with images of stick-n-poke tattoos. The photographs included in the collages were submitted to me via close friends and internet acquaintances. Tattoos, in essence, are a form of bodily affirmation, though stick-n-poke tattoos in particular are a hallmark of DIY queer punk identity. Stick-n-pokes do not use a machine; they often take longer and (some would argue) hurt more. Many of the submissions I received came with anecdotes along the lines of my best friend gave me this on a drunken night or I did this to myself in quarantine or my partner poked this. I chose to limit my collages to solely stick-n-poke tattoos as a way to honor these intimacies. A handful of the tattoos included in these collages were given to me by myself or were given by me to my loved ones. I am an honored facilitator of the particular joy that allows us to love our bodies even just a smidge more. The permanence and purpose of the practice is not lost on me—each tattoo stores the memory of who we are, who we were, and who we were with. My college roommate taught me the art of stick-n-poke tattoos during first-year orientation, as we embarked into the night with a pencil, thread, and sewing needle. The first full word I ever tattooed on myself: still. A reminder to stop shaking, to stay still. A reminder that I am still here, still breathing.

the fault is dead
& it is my spider

Resolution 279

On the way to work,
I am left
with no choice
but to jaywalk a highway
with two winding curves.

I daydream of being taken.

You can spot a rough day
by the way I keep my music playing,
without listening for the Death Machines—

Please
make no mistake,
the lady I work for
is splendid as s'mores,
it's the vacancy I carry
in my own sore eyes.

No, I didn't make any noise,
that was just the flat seltzer water
in my stomach. No,
I didn't cough. I gagged.
It's about time you all knew
of the pain in my elbow.

My mother wants to talk
about addiction but
I'm too sensitive &
singing has stopped
helping. My syntax is
—Forgive me,
have I forgotten
to surprise you?

Here is the part where
I peel back my skin
to show you just
how much
my muscles
ache. I'm about to snap
like a rubber band
having a heart attack.
Too much? I must
not speak
of the spider
in my throat.

Everyone
likes to tell me
what's a tickle
& what's a gash.
what's worth poems
& what's worth bandaids.
I say, Both. I say, Neither.

Why I Haven't Been Writing Poems Lately

there is an exhaust pipe resting in my open mouth / where the elegy is supposed to be / I hardly have time for lyric / between all this sleep / consider me a couchbound king / slouching / dressed in my best cheap satin set / like a cellar spider / curled in an unswept corner / feasting on mights but never moving / there are lines in my mind almost all of the time / night-blooming jasmine / moon-eyed arachnids / unpronounceable joy / my father's father's dust / I pause the poems / pick my face until it bleeds / think these hands used to have such elegant tasks / this tongue used to tap dance / now I get drunk on blue light / and too much time / I watch weeds rise in the rose garden / while the strawberries in the fridge / ripen red only to mold / mildewed by morning / my appetites fail me / maybe I am mourning / turning to pulp / waiting to molt / and metaphorize / the lack that is left of me

Spring Break for Suckers

Alone in a cabin
on Cemetery Street,
I find an excuse to ring
the whole family.
How are the wires
looking out west?
Home. Where
the heat is.

Down the road, there's a doll
in the window of a watermill,
abandoned. I am made up
of omens, made up omens.
Late March, still it snows
& the Northern Paper stings.

I crawl into a stranger
porcelain, clawfoot tub
with a belly of burnt cookies.
A part of me is bookmarked
there, dog-eared
in a memory, waiting
for poems to find me.

Scent of the season:
Marlboro Reds
& wool socks, wet.
Time traveling tobacco,
take me back, Oh!

Winter is over.
We vacuum up
the wasps.

Jorō Spider Cento

my East Coast friends
      tolerate a brief freeze
            while I / withstand
                  the palm of your hand

                I'm not prepared to say
         exactly how
     your hand, was
harmfully invasive

You / with spindly legs
      with a weakness for blood
            with a spatula or wooden spoon

            breaking human skin / me
      with bright yellow, blue and red coloration
actively being constrained

I / submit / and become / itsy-bitsy

that may sound like an extreme reaction,
but / I was
cornered
measured
compared
published
exposed
suited
climbed
squished
convinced
considered

a nuisance
for the following reasons:
I / sleep better at night
I'm / lovely / and / messy
and / learn / how / to live

kick / and / cause
significant disruptions

I / needed to get out of there

So / I don't / wind up missing
reports of someone
on the / news
woman or spider
with / golden silk
found / lying
like / prey on a riverbank
after / ambush

sympathizers are saying
        we should not draw sweeping conclusions
                there / were / no / signs of disturbing / behavior
                        Also, if / there were / our friend / was not involved
                She / may frighten people
        may even / be / [creepy / violent]
or (contrary to urban legend,)
        Venomous, but not dangerous
                not a threat, and there is no data to prove
                        she / is / guilty

So maybe consider / her heart
how the / blame / might be / long / to / you
were / you / even / sober
when / she / was / crawling on / you
were / you / already spread / and / draped
no
you shouldn't worry / you
should expect to come into close contact with / her
whether / you / want to or not
you / should take comfort in / all this
terrible / fear

it / was / inevitability / a / mistake

but / it sure felt like / no / accident
when / She / held / my / pulse
like a / wing / between / her / pincers
squeamish / with / slaughter

when / she said in an email
your / body / is a / basement
your / body / is a / pest
your / body / is a / thread
your / body / is an / invite
your / body / is a / bitten / fruit
your / body / is a / cigarette
your / body / is a / cheesecake
your / body / is a / sewer
your / body / is a problem

her / fangs / would likely scar me for life

I / begin / checking my legs
at both ends / taking / notice / of / each
ballooning / lump / and / throb
my / groin / and / joints / and / belly
turn / to / spectacle

poison
          in my
                    head

for / so / long
I / said / nothing

let / her / storm
and / sting / and
winter / my / spring

survival / is / a waiting game

The reality of the situation, though, is
horrifying / hunter
and / household pet
wanton / cannibalizing

I was / certain / to endure
would be / to / end

so / up the waterspout / I went
wed / to / web

courageously screaming
I'm / a / bride / to / the wind

at the intersection of

I am a victim & I
am
not
a
victim

I blink my bloodshots at strangers on the subway,
begging for them to notice
until they do.

I am so close to calling it what it is

abstruse / how obtuse / I was to her ruse /
despite bible induced / welts, profuse /

she bruised / my caboose / a bright chartreuse /
like rotten produce / I tried to refuse /

my voice reduced / to a cautious ooze /
a weaver, seduced / groomed to recluse /

afraid of her fuse / flambéed with booze /
too many brews / of vodka & juice /

there is no excuse / for the accused /
wretched muse / of my lingering blues /

I don't want this body, still haunted by

Sapphire

Had I stayed any longer,
I would have dissolved
like a Sweetart in soda.
Dull tongued,
become a synonym
for bruised.

I'm back now
& my body is thankless
for what we have survived
in silence.

You were the best thing
I ever left. Behind
me, a life
I am so glad I abandoned—
a life painful & lonely
& almost, broken neck
wailing in the bath,
days spent vacuuming ash.

Imagine her, the me I was,
the me you made
bleed through my long johns
my first winter a woman,
wounded with receipts.
Engaged at 18,
my finger swollen
& puke green
from the choking
ring.

The box beneath
my bed burns
sapphire, still

I am the brave
antonym of apology.

Amsterdam

There are as many reasons to stay
quiet as there are tulips in the Netherlands.

Ugly brained
in my negligee,
I wanted to shrink
to the size of a bicycle

basket. Hold only
the necessities: six dice,
a slice of cheese. I wanted
to wrap the canals

around my neck—slip through
the choke, become smoke.
Emptied of music
in the red light district,

I wanted to swallow
the whole Prinsengracht
but somewhere in me,
somewhere deep,

I knew I'd come back spitting
bright orange teeth.

my father was famous
for his paper roses
in the ward

Daughter of Worry

When Finnegan's underbelly sprouts
a new bump, we take him to the vet.
Beg for it to be benign. When my father
chokes a cough, seizes his thumb
to undo the spasm—
                    it is a lovely Sunday,
                    fit for a Bloody Mary.
I've been writing this poem
since the first grip
of diagnoses,
envisioning different ends.
The metaphor
remains:
The dogs have better healthcare than my father.

I am a daughter of worry.
His lungs are a museum of decay.
When the dander in my chest
developed into asthma,
he bought my inhalers
to disable his alarms.
Deflected care. *Recurring theme.*
                    He lights another cigarette

& I pretend
each sidewalk is an aisle
he is limping me down.
No one is promised
their rites of passage,
only passage. He dresses in black
every day, every day
he dresses in black.

In Place

When I visit my father
in the fluorescent wasteland
of my memory, I remember
him thinner than ever,
stubbled & smelling
of Irish Spring
& Marlboro Lights.

When I visit my therapist
in the fluorescent wasteland
of my memory, I remember
only the waiting
room, wood
frames & a television
that played *Snow White*
every time. I remember
the 7-Eleven across
the street, chock-full
of Lunchables
& the promise of after.

When I visit my brother & me
in that noonday memory,
I remember
      screen door slam,
sidewalk sunshine
as we left for the library,
      away from home.

I remember when I first remembered,
      I became the banshee tween
      of my twin sized bed
the flash flood of my father's blood.

I did not forgive forgetting,
until I learned the word
      repressing.

When I visited my father
in the Mental Hospital, I'm not sure
I knew it was a Mental Hospital.

     in that memory:
     my father's flannel
     on a floormate's back—

my father taking care
of someone else
in place
of himself.

Dear Brother

(who braved the brunt
for the both of us)
(who, stilted or stunted,
is still alive at twenty-five)
(who came out cord-caught
& kicking, miracle boy,
who came out singing Sinatra,
came out singing
Came Out Swinging,
who came out
tender as a bruise,
who bruises so easily,
like seriously, my tender-blooded
Von Willebrand brother,
King of the Block-
buster summer)
(who, in second grade, was shamed
for having nails painted flame—
who instead of going home,
& bathing in acetone,
inspired boys to do the same,
to steal their mother's polish
& paint, a protest in each shade
of pink, gold, green, blue)
(you, who protected me
from the torment of elementary,
who found me sobbing by the swing sets
& said, half-threat,
you'd hit the heels of
my bully with the sharp edge
of your Razor scooter, you,
who taught me tough skin,
never tormented again,
you, who still holds my hiccups with
the softest snarl, you)

(big brother, who cries beside me
at the Tigers Jaw concert, whole
decade later, whose life
was saved by songs
shouted in the shower,
shouted shrouded
in sweat, shouted silent
in the tourmaline night,
big brother, who gave me lyrics
like heirlooms for when the hurt hums
like heartbeats, like blueprints
of an architectured ocean
you tread & survived
—do it,
I dare you,
I triple dog dare
you, swim up straight
& admit that you're special.

This is how a sewing needle becomes a Saturday night

TO :

GAY  QUEER  TRANS  CHILDREN

TAKE NO SHIT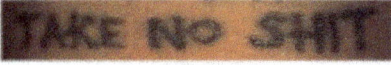

PURSUIT  JOY AND  the CRUSH

DON'T  Forgive  THE cruel  world  ,

SPIT  ON THE cruel  world  !

GIRL LOVE
IS
HALF CRUSH
HALF RISK
IS
the MODERN HOLY
the STILL STRANGE
STITCHED
JOY

ADORE

EVOLVES

INTO

LOVE

AS

SUMMER

EVOLVES

INTO

FALLING

 BARE

 BEFORE

 THE

 MIRROR

 SHE  TRIMS

 MY

 ARMPIT  HAIR

WE TANGLE
TONGUES IN
RASPBERRY
CHOCOLATE

TROPHALLAXIS

NAKED

EXCEPT FOR

OUR

WHISKEY COATS

I STROKE

THE

TICKLE

OF

YOUR BACK

 BODY

goodnight CRUEL BLUES

cuidate pain

i LOVE ME TENDER

TENDER tender

LOVE ME GENTLE

WILD AND STRANGE

(TRANS) Cowboy BITCH,

i'm HOLY.

P.S.

RISK the CRUSH

CHANCE MORE JOY

[please] be STILL

I research diagnoses
till the night is navy
blue, take a shot
of lavender oil
& wash my hair
with lighter fluid.

death lmao

is what i write when asked what keeps me up at night *death lmao* at the top of my list in comedy class *death lmao* among other things like the radiator and my bank account an empty swimming pool i am trying to stay afloat in *death lmao* is another way of saying my father my father is not dead but he's caught somewhere in the almost and i am almost always thinking about *death lmao* i knock on wood whenever it crosses my mind i have been looking for a pocket-sized plank for some time *death lmao knock knock* like the final hand in thirty-one which if you don't know is a card game i used to play with my grandmother who is alive just busy pouting and playing tennis my father *knock knock* has a bad knee and i can't picture him playing tennis or taking a walk but i can hear his cough *knock knock* no matter where i am *cough cough* carried between coasts like baggage or a bird *chirp chirp* when i first flew to boston my father came with me his only time out east and he couldn't believe all the brick and burial grounds *death lmao* my father spent his life *knock knock* working construction and smoking marlboros *cough cough* he wanted *knock knock* he wants cough cough to be an artist my father is an artist the kind that never sells anything while alive *death lmao* i imagine the estate sale i will one day have to have *knock knock* what does a daughter do with a collection of yard sticks and license plates sculptures and shot glasses *sláinte* means health but in my family *sláinte* means whiskey and whiskey means *death lmao* what does a daughter do with a garage full of dust cough cough lmao i take after my father dark brows and long lashes *blink blink* life flashes *blink blink* it is seventh grade *blink* it is senior year *blink* it is almost graduation and i am sleepless with *death lmao* though my bed frame is wooden *knock knock* i am at odds with the clock *tick tock* haunted by *cough cough cough cough* i used to think *blink blink* we had a pact *knock knock* not to surrender for the other's sake so from my poems i'd erase death and soften the edge *lmao* the ledge *lmao* with laughter like sandpaper my father *knock knock* taught me sláinte to take worry like whiskey and let it burn good *cough cough* to grin through the grit like a daughter should

Happy Birthday

1.
My mother calls & says
Thanks for calling.
Her love left.
She asked her love to leave.
She is cursed, she says.
She will die alone, she says.
I am too clanky for comfort.
I have a Zoom call in 13 minutes.
I let my silence multiply
until she can breathe.
Hang up. Tell her later
what Kim Addonizio told me:
listen I love you joy is coming
& it is easier to say
because the words are not mine.

2.
My father is making potato soup
& our milk is sour. The sky is gray
but I want to call it periwinkle.
It is mostly ash
& there is nothing
gorge about it.
At the cash register
with 2% & an It's-It, I think
I can't wait to walk here in two weeks
& buy blue tequila, Jäger, Straw-Ber-Rita, a vape—
anything to exacerbate
my asthmatic inhale,
my antihistamine exhaust.

3.
If you buy milk in hand-me-down
thrifted Prada boots
two sizes too big

41

& don't take a picture
because you don't want the men
on lawn chairs outside to know,
that you know, that sometimes,
in neon lights, when you can hardly breathe,
you are beautiful—

are you beautiful?

Resolution 362

I coughed
on my phone
& didn't keep
any promises.

Instead, I threw a birthday party
in my bathroom; nobody showed up.

[hyperbole owns my clock] OR [hyperbole took my future]

This moment is my forever.
I do not have a maker,
only the blood of angels.
We share Altoids & uncles.

I organize in piles
& forget to text Oma
back again. Advil & excuses.

My middle name is
a snake's wet dream.
I'll sew the two tips
of his tongue together
if he dare comes
whistling at me.

Use only earring wire
& lavender hand sanitizer.

Pop the pity champagne
I've kept at room temperature.

Stack. I see green
scales all over these
stanzas. Do your eyes
bleed apples also?

Crisp as cracking snow.
Sweet as sore legs.
Take what you mean
& run with it.

I ought to build a house of cards.

LA Overture

This morning,
the sewer water smelled
like butterscotch
& I found a beetle
flattened into the concrete
of Koreatown
Scooter vs. Scarab
squashed skid marks
shattering emerald
& on the escalator
leading down
to the 7th Street/Metro,
pigeons paint the handrails
splattering off-white,
flocks, lost
in the underground
ecosystem of delayed
train traffic & disappearances
but my sure step says
Not Me, Not Today
& my sure step says
Sure, You Can Ask Me for Directions
it's true, I do
know my way around
this angel angst town,
all its ins & outs
& In-N-Outs,
all the critters
between the cracks
gone off-track
& when your phone map
fails to find home,
wait for the bus
by a grate that pushes up
a hell of hot green-gray air,

—you're already there,
having a Marilyn Monroe moment
with the exquisite stink
spurting from the sidewalk's underbelly
& the truth is
the Silver Line is my favorite
sweat brigade but when the rush
hour crowd is too too much,
I turn the music up.
Los Angeles, I am not lonely with you
my love. The wires cutting
through the smog
wrap themselves around
my skittish heart
till I am electrocuted
by your current, watching
all the winged dreams around me
scribble footnotes in our city's story.

I promise to meet you there,
on the other end
of your night terrors—
where your howl
meets the perfumed air

femmes flirting

is like — here ,
take this playlist
          five hours of folk pop indie
& yearn
in the aubergine night
          to a dusty lullaby ;
tell me all the lyrics
that twinge your heart , sharp
& i will embroider them with thread
your favorite shade of red
(not quite carmine
          but close ,
like crimson ,
with a splash of cinnamon
more firebrick
          than blood)

femmes flirting is a flood
of paragraphs
exchanged each day ,
auto-caps-off , all lowercase
queering commas , we add a space
before every punctuation
to soften the end of our sentences
but our softness never ends ,
we bend
blue light into baby pink —
become sapphic memes , like
          do you think
          she likes me ?
like , it has only been five weeks
of *how'd you sleep ?*
and *sweet dreams*
the buzz of our phones : an ode ,
jolting me so jittery

so weak in the knees ,
a lamb could sneeze
& it'd knock me right out
as i write this , i drink
the breakfast tea she mailed me
from her corner of our sprawling city ,
a simmer on my tongue ,
a warmth brewing
in my butterfly belly —
the kiss she includes
inside the envelope
envelops me in mauve ,
strawberry stamped gloss

femmes flirting is
persistent tenderness ,
the perpendicular point .
where peppermint & lavender
oil meet — essential
essentially , a delicate mixology
of fragrance , the lingering haunt
of hands held , whole
holy , two bushes blooming
in jasmine joy

fuck — the world roughens us enough ,
so we love like egg yolks
in a vibrant gush , we love
like matchsticks , not gaslit
like chapstick ,
like why bruise what you could bandaid ?
we , femmes , make lemonade out of nightshade
my belladonna , mon cheri ,
my sugarbug , my chickadee ,
my fruit loop , my clementine ,
my tipsy kismet valentine

femmes flirting is the fluster ,
the cetaphil , the chorus of giggles ,
the bobby pins , the cricket hymns ,
moon pics & paperclips ,
the ampersands , the fallen wisps ,
the wine spills , the silk slips ,
the lipstick , the black lace ,
the velvet scrunchie , the knots of yarn ,
our secrets drenched in simile ,
our smiles , in spite & in spite & in spite

as she drinks water in the middle of the night, i wake to write this

3:32 AM

—the harsh clang of the cap, metal
kissing metal—like a child playing
with barbies except the barbies are
wearing steel toe boots and won't stop
kicking each other…like this
exactly but sweet, Swell

Canyon

"The love I've known is the love of / two people staring / not at each other, but in the same direction." -Frank Bidart

peak of the heat wave
& we're in a hot tub

watching bats circle above
us in the sherbet sky

this life of mine is beautiful
my past scorched to ash

& my heart beating again ,
like a phoenix , or better yet

the clumsy flap of bat wings
in Joshua Tree : it's our anniversary

& I am in love , I have entered love
I am sculpting a future out of butter

& guts allow me to get specific
we have a weekend together now

after months apart & I plan on
staring at you while you stare at me

breaking only when a bat flies by
so we can scrapbook the scene

in the album of our brain & replay
this particular this peculiar this life

we've cherished for some odd
hours (later, over oven-crisp

cauliflower fresh from the farmer's
market , we cross check all sixteen

species to identify the cauldron ,
the fluttering canyon fuzz

swirl diving in the dust
the fluster the buzz

surrounding us) they come
closest when we kiss

so we kiss until the water cools
& when we open our eyes ,

they swoop beside
our soaked straddle

before slipping into dusk
horizon-bound toward

that sliver of sun
behind the breeze-bent trees

& the tangle of wires
above our tangle of knees —

Wednesday: Erotic
after Audre Lorde

the event begins with cloud cake,
reaching for the remote
and pressing
pause, pressing
against the warm
weight of the other

until the need to press
furtherharderfaster
crescendos, devoured
by an urge desire built
from our soft valleys

it begins and begins again,
with a music only we can hear:
the rhythm of want
sounds in our ears

a lick
that flicks
a light switch

somewhere deep inside
my fingers plucking

the harp of your back

is enough to reach the edge
call it hunger, call it hanker

call it the mighty thirst
a pine tree on a cliffside
taking sips of the sky

building
up the courage
to ask for a gulp
oh! my only sunshine

a strand of your hair
flames me, ash
to a match,
you untame me
add kerosene

to the cause and
consequence to
the pause—now even
my piercing caught
in your tangled knots
is topaz.

love poem with allusion to *Cars 3*

I want to stick to you
like a June bug
on a summer night
dew to the lingering dawn
cricket to song
wet breath on silk heat
to heave like peppermint oil
kissing a cotton ball
dog hair to dark sheets
lint to wool socks
spilled lemonade
clinging to kitchen tile
like hotpot steamed
into crop tops
red onion rubbed tongue
smoke to flannel sleeves
Jolly Rancher to wrapper
& wine to teeth
like-like
blush to your cheeks

apricity
golden shovel, after The Wonder Years

Sunshine splintered in the bare skin of winter: Rare, like god
or a room temperature below blistering——the damn
radiator is broken so we sleep with the window open. You
snorehum, teeth clicking a harmony, & I drool a river on your pillow. We wake to look
at the snow collected on the sill. Sure, the night is holy
but the night is spent catching silverfish, sweating. The bed bathed
in eucalyptus & whisperwishes for sweeter dreams. There's nowhere I'd rather be than in
this blizzard heat, beside the steady breath of apricity, fidgeting on the
twin size mattress we somehow make work. It's the almost eve end of January
& I want to call you the brightest thing, but I won't, cause I'm wrong. We're right. You're light.

I am in the market
for new amazement &
anti-anxiety medication.
The doctor says
I don't have to live
in a battle with my body.
But my body is not a battle.
My body is a song
sung into the sink.

Yawn Song

I know my body
is real because
I ignore it everyday.
Shivering myself numb,
I say *The marine layer*
ate my poetry…faint
burps thick with fog.
I trust you understand
the difference between
fear and *mirror*—
a touch here, a
touch there. Come, please
find me murmuring
and chapped. Hickory
stiff sound as glass
slash an eyelash
        heavy
head   heavy
      head   heavy
        head
I never said I would make it
this far. I could bide
and stretch forever, I won't,
no reason why. It's almost
like the rest you need
gets in the way of the rest
you get—you get it.
My body is a box of tissues,
an empty jar on the edge
of a nightstand, night standing,
sleep walking. Or walking
while I should be sleeping.
Smoking, breathing. Graying,
teething.

I rise early each morning
to prove the day has worth,
but I move slow,
and dictionaries drown
as I drag my feet.

Berlin, without Return

after Voxtrot

I buried all my dresses
in donation bags because
wearing my body out
became too much of a drag

May

I apply hand sanitizer
before bed, afraid of my mouth

kissing my finger,
my finger kissing

the water fountain—
I've been checking

every pillow case
for spare laughter

maybe one day I'll learn
how to bleed

a radiator
all by myself

it's not summer until i watch Jersey Shore in the middle of the night

5:31 AM

and i hate it—i love it—i love to hate it
and i hate to love it—the men,
mostly, who talk like bulls in a pen,
kicking up sand, spitting out blood,
bucking and bucking in a frenzy of red
flags, yakking in the bathroom
while the women sob in the street,
sob under their covers, sob against the wall.
but i'm having fun—despite the violent flash
of images circling in my head—i'm having fun,
i'm enjoying myself, though i've spent
the past hour trying to kill a cupboard moth
that keeps disappearing—i baptize myself
in lavender oil, i resign, put down
the newspaper—and i know i need to sleep
but Sammie (the sweetest bitch you'll ever meet)
is about to discover The Letter and i want to watch
it happen, though i've seen it all before, every summer,
with my lights off, ceiling fan on, circling
and circling, shaking the still spring dust down
onto my duvet—eyes dry from allergies or eyes dry
from summer or eyes dry from staring at the miami strobe lights,
eyes dry and dizzy and it's comforting (but it's comforting,
but the scene is comforting) in the same way 2 AM is comforting,
that shade of summer blue, a sliver of light tinting the whole room
through a half-drawn blind, it's comforting though different now—
watching Jersey Shore, knowing what i know, living what
i lived.

August is the Cruelest Month

A piece of kale stuck
in the calendar's teeth.
Inky urchins where my
lungs should be. Sunburnt
scalp and sunburnt eyes:

unjustified. I had reapplied
several times, in a fight
with the rinse and wind—
still my ears blush to a crisp.
Is it superfish to complain
about a throbbing itch?

I don't want to get subcutaneous.
More convenient to write
a kitschy rhyme, rather than admit:
The curtains have been
drawn for weeks. Paranoia
sneaks, creeps, hurls
her pearls
       one
           by
               one
against the screen,
a bonus for each
agoraphobe she fashions.

Today, on the beach, I think
This shell looks a lot like me.
Wiped out metaphor. Easy
to read. The thing is—
too drab. I don't want to be
dour I want to make you laugh
and hardly no one yes no no one
asks are you—well—it's too sad.

Let's change the subject back.
I have been sleeping
with aloe on the nightstand.

If a girl cries with the door closed,
does her breath still smell of sour cream?

Ear Anecdotes

Mrs. Yonemura reports
I have selective hearing
in my parent-teacher conference.
I always finish my work
no matter how chatty
my table partner.
No matter the crunch
of the pencil sharpener.
Not even the laughter
rising by the window
could distract me
from my fractions.
It is fourth grade
& I already know
how to turn the world off.

I am raised on stage
beside the amplifier's
whine, the blurry dark
of an audience
in motion. My mother
insists we keep
earplugs in the glovebox
at all times. *You never know
where the night will take you.*
Rolling, rolling in her PT Cruiser:
ugly-cute chariot, from punk
show to punk show, across
the Southern California coast.
Somewhere, a toddler
in noise canceling headphones
is listening to Pennywise
from the inside out—
the bass drum
swells, shakes,
paints my bones
cobalt blue
with embarrassment.

In kindergarten,
I learn whispers
of a particular pitch
(right ear only)
tickle my lower spine
with a sharp sensation
my giggle-pangs
become a cherished
secret, one I share
only with lovers
& accidents
whisper, an arrow
into my back, a bow
plucked & arched.

                                    Slumber party &
                                    Sophie can't sleep
                                    unless—until
                                    the clock shuts up.
                                    Can't stand the incessant
                                    tick & *tock*
                                    I usually tune out,
                                    so we take it down
                                    unscrew each
                                    spiraling gear
                                    to build a fort
                                    of silence.

I'm convinced
my ears have super powers,
when Cleo pierces my lobe
with just ice & an apple
slice. I swap the post
the next day—there is no blood.

Child of caesura   (say *sorry*)
can't afford a real divorce,
so substitute: separation
& a symphony of
slamming doors.
Earbuds in & volume up,
crouched in a closet
corner.

Oma decides the antidote
for an unidentified
infection is tipping
a kettle down my canal,
boiled water
to flood the wax
that was never there.
She adds an ocean
to my sinuses
& stokes
the swimmer's ear.
I sob-splash all evening
till low tides return.

After an accidental slip
of cartilage in the Claire's gun,
my ache outlasts
every draft.
The burn begins,
turns almost vermilion.
Lopsided sleep,
I've been swollen ever since.
Spontaneity is like this:
defined by consequence.

I gave myself
the swimmer's
sequel, head tilted
into microwaved
tap water. Homemade
saline, salt soak
without solution—

Most mornings,
I wake to the sound
of my father gagging.
Unfortunately ordinary,
an echo through the living
room. I listen to
automated rain & pretend
I am in yesterday.

Nicknamed bionic
by Cathy, who claims
no whisper is safe
when I am at the other
end of the hall
even now
I hear her
in the kitchen
telling my father
all about—

How did I not hear
my brother
in the next room
standing on a cliffside?

Pulsing with pus
where the piercing went
wrong, that whole year
my ear marked
a blood dried boundary.
Don't hug. Don't fuck. Don't touch.
Ruby to rust,
the power shifts.
I was in charge
of my own bark
& wince.

Tiffany, in October,
at the end
of our week-
long sleepover,
asks me to return
the captive bead
to her cartilage hoop.
Holding her ear
between my fingers,
I roll her helix
into place &
kiss her, whisper
until winter.

We make love on a bar of chocolate,
on accident, on a duvet
now smothered in Ghiradelli
glee! We stain her sheets
with intense dark raspberry
& the laughter we share
is its own kind of lovemaking.
She washes my back
while we shower together,
soap rinsing where
I can't reach, skin
sticky with sugar
smooshed mid-smooch
& it becomes unclear
whether the smudge
behind my left ear
is a remnant of our
wet wrestle, or a mole
I had gone my whole life
without noticing—
she licks the spot
strawberry
vodka on her
breath, to ensure
I taste like myself.

I hear what I can
through the waves.
        If I stopped the silence I'd break.
Reverse osmosis,
dilute the dismal.
I can't drown today
I do not listen to my father
wrangle his cough in the night
& the texts I collect
pass my mind
but I haven't the time
to hear back. Blistered
bits fill my brain;
there is no choice
but to erase.

I   hear
in

            fractions

            the world

                                                    's
                                  whine

                            rolling

                                        inside

                                              blue

whispers

Child   *sorry*

                              &

                              closet

74

sob

Homemade

rain

I am

on a cliffside

with

a blood dried

bark

as

I   listen
                    in the night
&
          mind

The woman in me left
like the last drop
wrung from a washcloth

Wordum Wrixlan

At eighteen,
impulse & daydream
divided by silkscreen.

The commute to Cheever
is two miles of blind spots,
rounded up.

Each walk,
I want the wind
in the road to make ice

out of me—
stutter into
stained glass.

I write to keep
from spiraling, spinning, drifting,
dancing into traffic.

At twenty-two,
the urge to disappear
disappears

& Oma asks
where the poems have gone.
I show her the steady weaver,

yanking sunlight from inside,
scribbling threads
to swallow at dawn.

Patient as an ocean
brought to boil.
Still still.

Acknowledgements

My gratitude to the following publications, in which these poems first appeared:

Blue Marble Review — "Dear Brother"

Poetry Online — "In Place" and "*death lmao*"

The Somerville Times — "Wordum Wrixlan"

Summertime: Odes to LA — "LA Overture" and "femmes flirting"

The Wellesley Review — "apricity"

To the lighthouse that is Dan Chiasson (who once said *poetry is how we beat back the panic*—), thank you for beaming through the gray and illuminating my way.

To Tavi, with hope that every queer kid has a professor like you, who taught me joy is a protest and rage is an exclamation point, thank you for asking *where are all the long poems?*

To Kathleen Brogan, who cares about the teeniest of commas, thank you for Poetics of the Body.

To Thomas Nolden, whose humor brings out the best in every student, thank you for showing me Berlin right before the world changed forever.

To Frank Bidart, thank you for queering em dashes and giving titles to my poems.

To William Cain, who calls everyone a friend and means it, your incalculable enthusiasm reminds me to write with awe.

To Cleo, the worm to my rainy sidewalk, thank you for being the very best a best friend can be.

To Pixie, whose friendship has carried me throughout the years, thank you for the laughter and long drives (the aux is yours forever).

To Kelly Grace Thomas and the little pink classroom that started it all, thank you for waking up the poet in me.

To my dearest Oma, with hope that I have made you proud, thank you for the San Mateo summers and all the memories I cherish: stacks of quarters on the card table, Costco pizza, Splish Splash blasting in your bright red buggy.

To my brother, who does not get enough credit for his brilliance, thank you for introducing me to John Cusack and The Wonder Years, for finishing my leftovers and always looking out for me.

To Janet, the sister I never had and always wanted, thank you for the generous love and the wackiest niblings, Noodle and Bean.

To my mother, who is as kind as I am caffeinated, thank you for doing what you had to do.

To my father, a sea spider (I'll explain), thank you for listening to my every whine and wonder.

To Katrina, Cathy, Shelley, Olga, and the whole entire Cuda/O'Neil/Gagnon/Zimmerman family, thank you for being such a stylish, supportive bunch.

To Gabby, Michaela, Audrea, Grace, Bryn, Archie, Katherine, Jenn, Jasmine, Kris, Alex, Sri, Emma, Alexa, Lakota, the *Summertime* crew, and all my beautiful, beautiful friends, thank you for coaxing this hermit crab out of her shell.

To everyone who answered the call to send me their stick-n-pokes, thank you for trusting me with your chosen words.

To the many muses, mentors, and mentees whose heartbeats are sewn into the pulse of my poems, thank you for the soul salves and direction.

To my beloved blurb-gifters Nnenna Loveth Nwafor, Marcos James, and Matthew Cuban, thank you for capturing this collection with such care.

To Josh Savory (the GOAT), Ally Ang, and all the folks at Game Over Books who helped make this moment happen, thank you thank you thank you. There is no team I would trust more.

To you, reader, how lucky am I that someone as cool as you might pick up these poems?

To every queer kid, survivor, emo teen, and arachnid enthusiast, I love you.

To Tiffany, my whole heart and honeypot ant, yes! I will fill your water bottle ♡ I will tie ribbons to your plaits in the most treacherous wind. I will rest my palm between your shoulder blades so you can sleep sweetly.

Biography

Mila Cuda is a caffeine-sensitive lesbian from Los Angeles with an unmatched enthusiasm for spiders. The former Youth Poet Laureate of the West Coast, her work has been featured on Teen Vogue, Button Poetry, Rookie, PBS and Poetry Online. A two-time winner of The Charlotte Paul Reese Memorial Prize for Creativity in Poetry, she now lives in Somerville, MA, with her partner and the seasons. Still (Game Over Books, 2024) is her first full-length collection.